CROSS-SECTIONS

THE A-10
THUNDERBOLT

by Ole Steen Hansen
illustrated by Alex Pang
Consultant: Craig Hoyle, Defense Editor, Flight International

Capstone
press
Mankato, Minnesota

First published in the United States in 2006 by Capstone Press
151 Good Counsel Drive, P.O. Box 669, Mankato, Minnesota 56002
http://www.capstonepress.com

Library of Congress Cataloging-in-Publication Data
Hansen, Ole Steen.
    The A-10 Thunderbolt / by Ole Steen Hansen ; illustrated by Alex Pang.
    p. cm.—(Edge books, cross-sections)
    Summary: "An in-depth look at the A-10 Thunderbolt, with detailed cross-section
diagrams, action photos, and fascinating facts"—Provided by publisher.
    Includes bibliographical references and index.
    ISBN 0-7368-5251-4 (hardcover)
    1. A-10 (Jet attack plane)—Juvenile literature. 2. Airplanes, Military—United
States—Juvenile literature. I. Pang, Alex, ill. II. Title. II. Series.
UG1242.A28H36 2006
623.74'63—dc22   2005009632

Designed and produced by

David West Children's Books
7 Princeton Court
55 Felsham Road
Purney
London SW15 1AZ

Designer: Gary Jeffrey
Editors: Gail Bushnell, Kate Newport

Photo Credits
Corbis, 28/29, Flight International, 6-7; U.S. Airforce photo, 1, 5, 6, 10t, 18, 20, 21,
23, 29; U.S. Navy photo by photographer's mate second class Daniel J Mclain, 20

1 2 3 4 5 6 10 09 08 07 06 05

TABLE OF CONTENTS

THE A-10 THUNDERBOLT II

The A-10 Thunderbolt II was built to help soldiers on the ground and to crush enemy tanks. The A-10 is not as fast as other jets. But it is one of the deadliest ground attack aircraft in the world. It can carry a huge weapons load to use on the enemy.

The A-10 was first made in the 1970s and is nicknamed the Warthog. A-10 pilots have a saying about their aircraft: "Never wrestle with a Warthog. You will both get dirty, but the Warthog loves it!"

GROUND ATTACK AIRCRAFT

During World War II (1939–1945), fighters were often needed to help troops on the ground. This need led to the idea of building ground attack aircraft.

THE P-47 THUNDERBOLT

The P-47 fought enemy fighters in the air during World War II. P-47s were also given bombs and rockets to use against enemy guns, trucks, and tanks.

The P-47 was the first U.S. fighter to be called Thunderbolt. Today the A-10 is the Thunderbolt II.

A-1 SKYRAIDER

The Skyraider was slow, but it was easy to turn. It was also able to stay over the battlefield for much longer than the fast jets.

In the Vietnam War (1954–1975), heavily armed Skyraiders were used to keep the enemy away from pilots who had been shot down.

HENSCHEL HS 129

The Henschel Hs 129 was used by the Germans during World War II. It could be fitted with a big gun to crush enemy tanks. This heavy weapon made the aircraft difficult to fly, but it took only one hit from its gun to stop an enemy tank.

The Hs 129 was the world's first aircraft made especially for destroying tanks.

CROSS-SECTION

Take a look inside the Warthog. The labels show which pages will help you find out more.

World War II ground attack aircraft gave their crews very little protection from the enemy. The A-10 was built to give its pilot a much better chance of staying safe. Everything on the aircraft is carefully planned to help it to do its job.

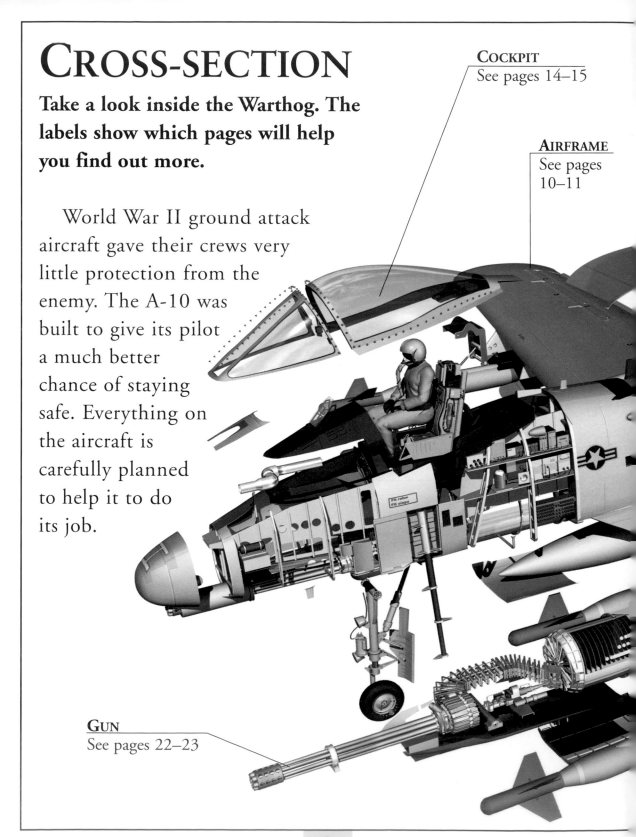

COCKPIT
See pages 14–15

AIRFRAME
See pages 10–11

GUN
See pages 22–23

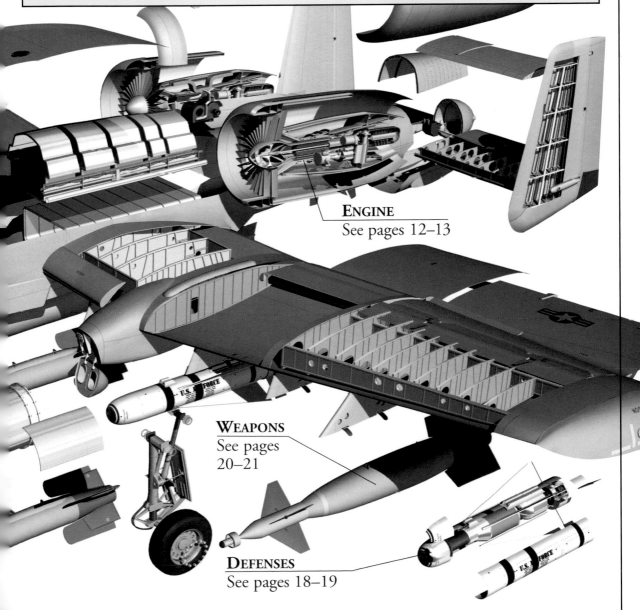

A-10 THUNDERBOLT II
Wingspan: 57 feet, 6 inches (17.5 meters)
Length: 53 feet, 4 inches (16.3 meters)
Height: 14 feet, 8 inches (4.5 meters)
Maximum speed: 420 miles
(676 kilometers) per hour
Maximum weapons load: 16,000 pounds
(7,250 kilograms)

ENGINE
See pages 12–13

WEAPONS
See pages
20–21

DEFENSES
See pages 18–19

THE AIRFRAME

The airframe of the A-10 is made to be very strong. The aircraft can still fly even if a tail fin or an engine has been damaged or destroyed.

The A-10's long, straight wing is good at giving lots of lift. The extra lift allows the A-10 to carry a heavy load. But the wing is not designed for high speeds.

The A-10 can fly slowly enough to take off from and land on short runways.

The straight wing helps the A-10 to turn sharply. It can turn more easily than many faster jets.

The A-10's wheels do not fully retract. This protects the airframe in case of a wheels-up landing.

THE ENGINES

The A-10 has two engines. A large fan at the front pushes large amounts of cold air back around the rest of the engine.

This kind of jet engine is called a turbofan. It is very quiet and uses very little fuel.

The hot air from the Warthog's exhaust is wrapped in cold air. Cooling the exhaust makes it difficult for any heat-seeking enemy missiles to locate the hot engines.

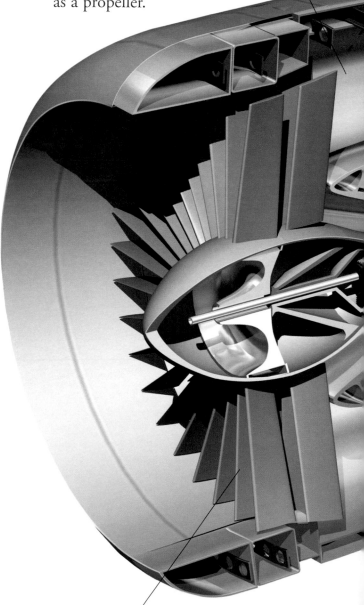

BYPASS DUCT
Some of the air for the fan is pushed through the bypass duct. So the fan partly works as a propeller.

AIR INTAKE
Air is sucked in by large fans at the front of the engine.

ENGINE SPECIFICATIONS
Two General Electric TF34-GE-100 each weighing 9,065 pounds (4,112 kilograms)

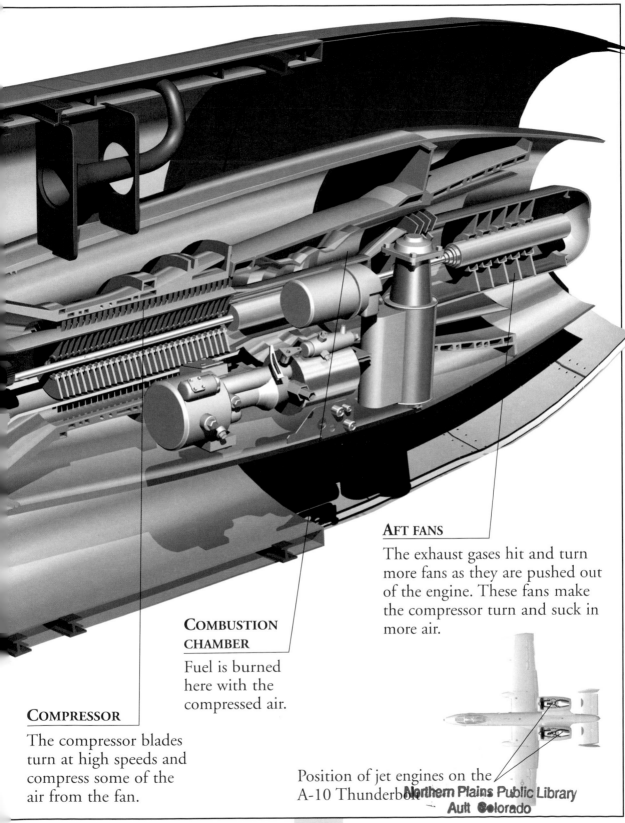

AFT FANS

The exhaust gases hit and turn more fans as they are pushed out of the engine. These fans make the compressor turn and suck in more air.

COMBUSTION CHAMBER

Fuel is burned here with the compressed air.

COMPRESSOR

The compressor blades turn at high speeds and compress some of the air from the fan.

Position of jet engines on the A-10 Thunderbolt

THE COCKPIT

The cockpit is made to keep the pilot as safe as possible. The A-10's missions often involve flying at low level. An enemy soldier with a gun could fire at the aircraft.

KEY TO DIAGRAM
1. Control stick
2. Rudder pedals
3. Throttle
4. Altimeter (shows the plane's height)
5. Airspeed indicator
6. Speed of climb
7. Radar display
8. Compass
9. Head-up display (HUD)

The cockpit canopy is bulletproof. The glass plate on top of the instrument panel is the head-up display (HUD). The HUD gives the pilot information on airspeed, altitude, and targets without having to look down at the instrument panel.

The cockpit is built into an armored "bathtub" made from titanium. It protects the pilot against shells that can pierce armor.

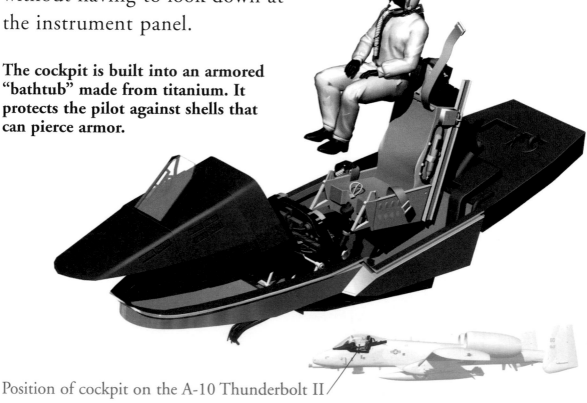

Position of cockpit on the A-10 Thunderbolt II

A-10 AVIONICS

Electronic systems in aircraft are called avionics. The avionics help the A-10 to find its way and to fight.

The Global Positioning System (GPS) tells pilots where they are and where they are going. The LASTE-system warns pilots if they are close to hitting the ground. It also helps them aim their bombs.

During a battle, a pilot needs to know exactly where friendly and enemy forces are. In the diagram, an A-10 has been hit and has made a crash landing.

3. The A-10 guards the airspace around the downed aircraft.

Position of avionics in the A-10 Thunderbolt II

RADAR WARNING RECEIVER – warns the pilot when an enemy radar has spotted his aircraft

PAVE PENNY LASER – for aiming weapons

RADIO ANTENNAS – to stay in contact with ground units or other aircraft

2. The AWACS calls in another A-10 to keep the enemy away from the downed aircraft.

4. A rescue helicopter arrives at the crash site quickly and safely.

1. Before it crashed, the A-10 told an AWACS radar aircraft what was happening.

DEFENSES

The Warthog must be well protected against enemy missiles. Both heat-seeking and radar-controlled missiles can be used against an A-10.

Enemy soldiers on the ground can fire shoulder-launched missiles against aircraft. These missiles are heat-seeking and target the A-10's hot engines. They cannot travel very far, but enemies can hide anywhere with this type of missile. Radar-controlled missiles can be controlled by radar on the ground or in an enemy fighter.

Chaff is metal foil that spreads out behind the A-10 to confuse a radar-controlled missile.

Flares are fired against heat-seeking missiles. The intention is that the missile will explode among the hot flares and miss the engine.

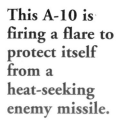

This A-10 is firing a flare to protect itself from a heat-seeking enemy missile.

Radar-based missile

Chaff sent out from wingtip

Heat-seeking missile

Flares sent out from landing gear sponsons

A jammer pod gives out signals that confuse the enemy radar. The enemy fighter will not be able to "see" the A-10, and the enemy radar-controlled missile will not be able to hit it.

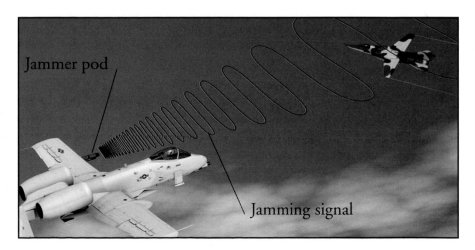

Jammer pod

Jamming signal

THE PAYLOAD

The Warthog can carry many missiles and bombs. The plane carries a selection on each mission, depending on what must be done.

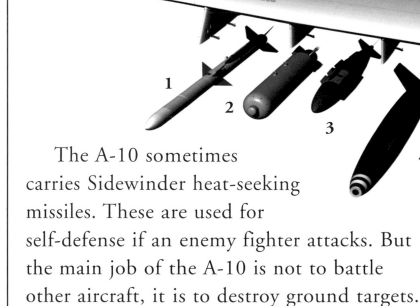

The A-10 sometimes carries Sidewinder heat-seeking missiles. These are used for self-defense if an enemy fighter attacks. But the main job of the A-10 is not to battle other aircraft, it is to destroy ground targets.

The ground crew is carefully trained to fit missiles onto the A-10 as quickly and as safely as possible.

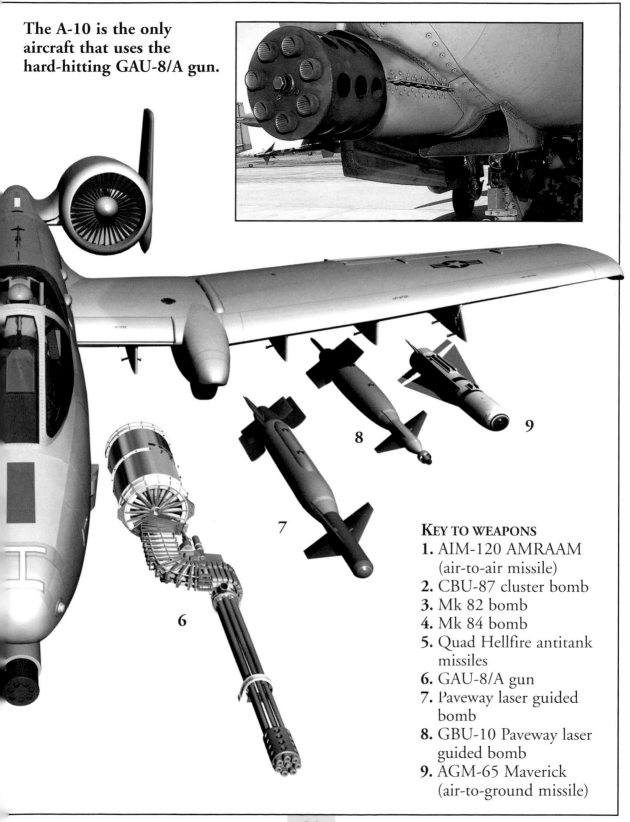

The A-10 is the only aircraft that uses the hard-hitting GAU-8/A gun.

KEY TO WEAPONS
1. AIM-120 AMRAAM (air-to-air missile)
2. CBU-87 cluster bomb
3. Mk 82 bomb
4. Mk 84 bomb
5. Quad Hellfire antitank missiles
6. GAU-8/A gun
7. Paveway laser guided bomb
8. GBU-10 Paveway laser guided bomb
9. AGM-65 Maverick (air-to-ground missile)

THE GUN

The GAU-8/A 30 mm machine gun is the most powerful gun ever flown in an aircraft.

The A-10's gun fires up to 4,000 rounds per minute. The shells are tipped with depleted uranium, a very heavy metal. These heavy shells fly through the air at high speed and cut easily through all armor. Once inside an enemy tank, the uranium shells burst into flame and set the tank on fire.

The gun must be in the center of the aircraft. When it fires, the force acts as a brake. The aircraft would start to turn if the gun were not in the center.

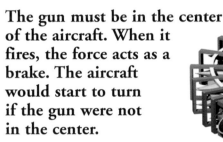

SEVEN-BARREL GUN MUZZLE

Position of gun on A-10 Thunderbolt II

LONG GUN

The GAU-8/A is 22 feet (6.7 meters) long. The barrels alone are 7.6 feet (2.3 meters). The shells fly at 3,399 feet (1,036 meters) per second when they leave the muzzle.

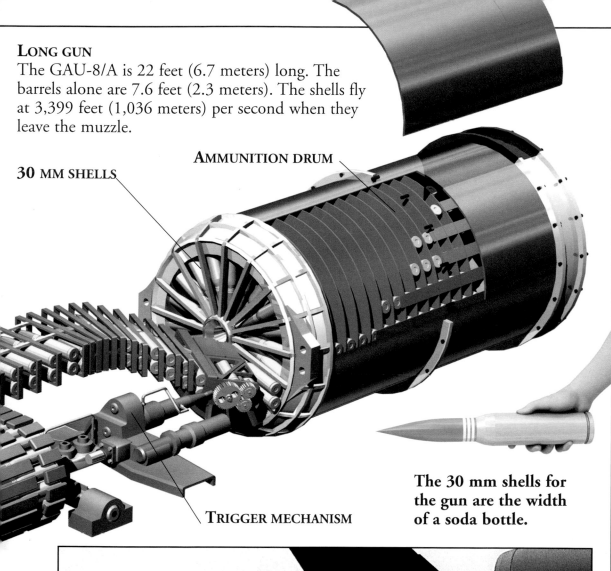

AMMUNITION DRUM

30 MM SHELLS

TRIGGER MECHANISM

The 30 mm shells for the gun are the width of a soda bottle.

When the gun is fired, the A-10 shakes and vibrates. Gun smoke spreads around the cockpit and the noise can be heard for miles.

SMART WEAPONS

Smart weapons can hit targets that are long distances away. This makes it much easier to attack an enemy without getting into danger.

The A-10's most useful weapon against tanks is the AGM-65 Maverick. It has a television seeker at the front. It sends a picture to the A-10 pilot. The pilot uses the screen in the cockpit to aim and fire the missile. The missile can also have an infrared seeker so that it can even find targets hidden under camouflage by picking up the heat of their engines.

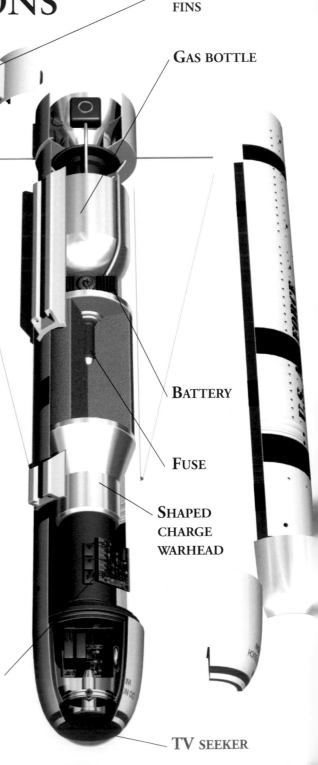

GUIDANCE FINS

GAS BOTTLE

BATTERY

FUSE

SHAPED CHARGE WARHEAD

ELECTRONICS

TV SEEKER

MAVERICK
The A-10 can carry up to 10 AGM-65 Mavericks.

GBU-10 PAVEWAY

The GBU-10 smart bomb is a 2,000-pound (900-kilogram) freefall Mk 84 bomb. Its guidance system is designed to be aimed from a distance.

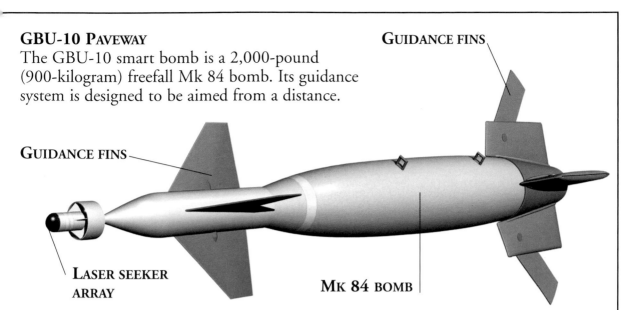

GUIDANCE FINS

GUIDANCE FINS

LASER SEEKER ARRAY

MK 84 BOMB

A soldier on the ground or in another aircraft can point out the target using a laser designator. The A-10 picks up the laser beams and aims its smart bombs at them.

This Warthog is firing an AGM-88 HARM anti-radar missile.

THE MISSION

The Warthog is mainly used to attack enemy troops and to help friendly troops on the ground.

A-10s have played an important role in recent wars in the Middle East and the Balkans. Their job often involves flying at a low level, which is dangerous.

Pictured here is a typical A-10 mission against enemy ground forces.

5. One A-10 has been hit in an engine. The pilot shuts an engine down and is able to return safely to base on one engine.

1. Two A-10s take off armed with Maverick antitank missiles. They also carry Sidewinder missiles for self-defense if they meet enemy aircraft.

4. The A-10s attack. They use their guns and missiles to fire at the tanks. The enemy tanks then return fire with their guns.

3. The OA-10 tells the A-10s where the enemy tanks are. The two A-10s split up, ready to attack from different sides to confuse the enemy.

2. The A-10 can also be used as a spotter plane, called an OA-10. This OA-10 has sighted some unidentified tanks. The pilot checks with the ground forces that they are not friendly tanks.

THE FUTURE

The A-10 Thunderbolt II will stay in service until 2028. By then it will have been around for 53 years.

The Warthog was planned as an aircraft that could fly low and close to enemy tanks. It can fly slowly over enemies for a long time waiting to crush them.

New smart weapons mean that enemy forces can be destroyed from higher altitudes and longer distances. The F-16 Fighting Falcons are newer aircraft that are better suited to this job. In the future, the A-10 will be used as a spotter plane.

The A-10 is an excellent spotter aircraft. It can circle over the battlefield for a long time.

28

New avionics and weapons will keep the A-10 up to date.

Glossary

armor (AR-mur)—a protective metal covering

bulletproof (BUL-uht-proof)—made to protect people from bullets

chaff (CHAF)—strips of metal foil released into the air to confuse a radar-controlled missile

exhaust (eg-ZAWST)—heated air leaving a jet engine

flare (FLAIR)—a sudden burst of light and flames; Warthogs fire flares to confuse heat-seeking missiles.

infrared (in-fruh-RED)—able to find objects by picking up traces of heat

mission (MISH-uhn)—a task given to a person or group

radar (RAY-dar)—equipment that uses radio waves to find or guide objects

retract (rih-TRAKT)—to pull back inside a covering; the Warthog's wheels do not retract fully but always stick out a small amount in case of an emergency landing.

READ MORE

Green, Michael, and Gladys Green. *Close Air Support Fighters: The A-10 Thunderbolt IIs.* War Planes. Mankato, Minn.: Capstone Press, 2004.

Hansen, Ole Steen. *Air Combat.* The Story of Flight. New York: Crabtree, 2004.

Jefferis, David. *Aircraft.* Pockets. New York: DK, 2004.

Shuter, Jane. *War Machines.* Military Vehicles Past and Present. Travel through Time. Chicago: Raintree, 2004.

INTERNET SITES

FactHound offers a safe, fun way to find Internet sites related to this book. All of the sites on FactHound have been researched by our staff.

Here's how:
1. Visit *www.facthound.com*
2. Type in this special code **0736852514** for age-appropriate sites. Or enter a search word related to this book for a more general search.
3. Click on the **Fetch It** button.

FactHound will fetch the best sites for you!

INDEX